HUMAN CICADA

Human Cicada
Copyright ©2022 by Carlos Cumpián

Prickly Pear Publishing & Nopalli Press
Santa Fe, New Mexico
pricklypearpublishing.com

First Edition, Printed in the United States of America
Library of Congress Control Number: 2022900005
Cumpián, Carlos.
Human Cicada/Carlos Cumpián
ISBN 978-1-889568-10-2 (pbk.)
I. Title.
Chicano Poetry, Indigenous Native American, Mexican-American Texas, Chicago.

Book Design: Qais Yahia Assali
Cover Photography ©: Cynthia L. Gallaher

ISBN 978-1-889568-10-2

Acknowledgements

The following wonderful souls present and passed on to the next stage: My relatives José Correa, John Correa, Alicia & Justo Correa, Orlando "Blackie" Correa, Dimas Correa, Francisco & Francis Correa, Aurora Correa Ochoa, Mary Lou Salazar, Jesusa Correa, Maria B. Gonzalez Cumpián, Miguel A. Cumpián, José G. Cumpián, Ramiro G. Cumpián, Estella Tyson, Ricardo Muñoz, Ramon & Jesusa Flores, la familia de Leonardo Villanueva, Beto Galán, ~

Amigos & compas: William Bill Finchum, E. Donald Two-Rivers, William Oandasan, Marianna & Carlos A. Cortez Koyokuikatl, Eugene Nelson, Rey Vasquez, Raúl R. Salinas, Jesus Chuy Negrete, Clayton Eshleman.

The following living individuals encouraged me to stay on the poetry path: Professor Marc J. Zimmerman, Al DeGenova, Raúl Niño, Sandra Cisneros, José Bono, Antonio Zavala, Luis J. Rodriguez, Gina Gamboa, Denise Dee Sweet, Ana Castillo, Carlos Morton, Frank Varela, Armando Rendon, Brenda Cardenas, David Ranney, Don Evans, Ernesto T. Mireles, Frank T. Blazquez, José Luis Benavides, Marta Ayala, Michael L. Liebler, Monica R. Rico, Rita Rousseau & Negrete sisters, David Schein, TAPESTRY, Outdoor Café reading series Tom Roby & Jenene Ravensloot, Guild Complex magic couple Mary Hawley & Mike Puican, Lisa Kay Adam, Richard Vargas, Sal Vega, Vittorio Ciummo, Colleen Springer-Lopez of CABE, Xanath Caraza and my loving family.

A special abrazo to poet Odilia Galván Rodríguez, who has made Prickly Pear Publishing an oasis.

To Lucy

Carlos Campian

2022

Mi]u...ee

Dedicated to the "tap pilam/earth humans" ancestors:
apkuētukuē apāxāi santcē wasāyaxām/
it will never be extinguished.

Contents

Travelers Without Maps

Almost Invisible Talents

Heroics and Misery Cults

TRAVELERS WITHOUT MAPS

Metztli Tochtli*

Sky neighbor monthly orbits, hides, seeks,
labors in fullness, crescent and shadows,
Luna observes our home as it
fluctuates from aqua turquoise blue to
snow-owl white, yucca-blossom yellow,
caramel-fungal brown to dusty wool
red sands, below grey-slate mountain
ranges & green rhizome lands —

Eyes rise off this stone spot
here in the Southern isthmus —
while our planet's many millenniums-old
companion also changes under gossamer clouds,
a sheer scarf moves across silvery surface,
briefly revealing Luna's rabbit-tochtli
crater tattoo that is seen in bright contrast.

*Metztli is moon & tochtli is rabbit in Mexican Nahuatl

Island Time

Frogs stir in dark huddles
riding concentric circles
of each ambassadorial rain drop
sent from Tlaloc, rain guardian of
Mexicans, or Chac Mool of Mayans.

At dawn's cerulean light the ceremony starts,
we wake up to island breaths and beats that consist
of calliope's mixture of muddy whistles and squeaks
like a thousand marching tiny rubber boots,
an occasional undercurrent high pitch riff carries
echoing quacks of a prehistoric duck eclipsed
when local roosters do their tropical call and response,
a dozen West Indian canticles announce
yesterday's April full moon departure.

Tree parrots' squawks blend with mourning doves
cooing, as their little winged neighbors,
banana finches and hummingbirds,
flutter under the foliage of baobab tree,
just add the bray of an occasional donkey
wandering some calmative high road on island time,
and this is morning traffic St. John style.

Last Concert at Rivendell*

After sun descends and moon climbs the darkening sky,
slowly she breaks through a gallery of clouds to inspire
an inescapable choir of ten-thousand invisible tree inhabitants –
their opus begins in a gabble as a beaded rain saturates the air.

July's warm breezes carry the incessant stirring,
striking similar to gourd rattles strapped to calves and ankles
of Mexica dancers moving in unison, going past pain
where exhaustion would be normal, as decibels soar.

An additional layer of deer antlers rub together
against stands of old bark clusters of wooded Yellow-poplar,
Witch Hazel, Hickories, Hawthorns, Hackberry, Red Maples.

The seed bead percussionists hold vigil outside our windows
while hungry bats swoop in and around the grounds,
the night's verdant blanket over Tennessee woods
cools as summer's earth insects' orchestra play on.

*The Rivendell Writers' Colony outside the city of Sewanee, Tenn., closed in 2018.

Vermillion Map

We local birds know the Dakotas,
just fly and follow the Missouri River or, as we heard
it said in Lakotayapi, follow the Waséoyuze out —
the place where Vermillion is.

French men came looking for bargains seeking the best
bison furs and beaver pelts, they sounded funny but left us alone,
later, other white settlers showed up and stayed to chop down
our valley of trees, taking away old homes.

Maybe it was John James Audubon's fault that Vermillion
was put on the map – a map that should only line the
cages for their starlings, those aggressive imitators always
threatening us indigenous birds who Audubon came to see.

Starlings showed up in droves from mossy castles
and pig smelly villages, it was better
when we were once separated by a vast cold ocean,
but they landed and built battlement nests upon their arrival.

Vermillion's starlings never learned our tunes,
the songs we have sung since Golden-Crowned Kinglet antiquity,
our songs sung while perched on the backs of bison nations,
who pounded out paths in the once open prairies.

Chupacabra Furlough

For Marc Zimmerman

Wake up, loco, it's just after six
in the morning, my Tejano connections
yesterday sent me some impeccable proof
from the Lower Rio Grande Valley.

Attached is a plethora of film footage, it's what
we've been waiting for because experts found
no image manipulation of this elusive fast-footed
creature now captured on a sheriff's dashboard camera.

Deputies Zavala and Dulce Mora of Falfurrias
offered indispensable first-hand testimonies,
even a notarized statement came
from poet priest Raúl Niño de San Benito.

I think we're beginning to agree
esté chiquito Chupacabra is no more mito
than you or me. It's no fable, neither
unicorn nor minotaur,

Nor is it some hydra-headed Argus from days of yore,
this ain't no Monterrey-mountain-top flying bruja
causing a piss-cop rookie to camera cry
on tele's *primera impacto.*

We know the critter's etymology comes straight from Spanish
with Latin roots, for to suck is *chupar* and *cabra* is goat.

Question numero uno, is where did this diablo come from?
Where indeed did this beast first appear – was it on

the Caribe Island of Borinquen, or do you still say Puerto Rico?
Did we forget its initial reports, how this creature dashed around
old Rich Port with the speed of a swiftly pitched baseball,
until one night, when people on an old jibaro's farm all

Stopped still in their tracks to witness the yet-unclassified beast
tapping a liquid meal out of a skinny goat's neck.
It's as if some strange hurricane flung this crypto-species
critter out from the bowels of deepest Africa

With no documentation, always on furlough
from the annals of discoveries,
this genetic cul-de-sac just appeared,
all weird dog and Komodo dragon-like,

With bristles and quarry-ripping claws, red-eyed
and ready to roam off shore, "Coño scary perro!"
some barrio kids said, when pictures and drawings
appeared in San Juan's news the next day.

Relax gente, we're safe in Humboldt Park,
(but watch out Hyde Park) por que esa sucker
wouldn't find enuf blood to live on after Chicago's
mosquitoes do their picnicking in July.

Fort Worth, Texas

Maria tells it como a si,
cuando ese Phil Felipe
el gaucho en botas rojas
era bien tonto back in April, 1994
got into his prontomoblie—a Saab,
took his seat belt off allowing
panza pounds to move around
now without constraints and
not wanting to be late, he lead-footed the gas
pedal for his next night's dinner date
but he wacked a pothole the size of a
small horses' drinking trough which
broke his rusty axle, so he was
forced to push his ride across
the interstate from seven PM
to ten—lucky it never rained.

He got where he wanted to be
on board the eastern bound plane at 1:AM
to rub shoulders with destiny—
walking straight up the aisle
in tight formation wearing a navy
linen jacket came the truffle of his life on heels,
she saw his conflicted smile and wanted
to sooth the sadness eating away at his traveler's soul,

Felipe in cowboy boots lost his balance
while sitting down and bumped her with his shoulder.
She didn't know his name but said, "Watch it
Honey," boldly he wanted to ask her for her handle
what did she go by and where was she flying solo?

She told him to bury her father who wrote for
The New York Times, a virus struck him a week ago
with those words, he felt he'd face troth damnation
if he didn't get her digits and her full name.

To expand the situation –she asked him if he would
be a darling and help her move her dad's coffin
at the luggage arrival terminal and get it into
her rented van when she drove around.

She made mention after they locked their seat belts
while moving toward the exit that she had a fever and
feeling cold, he wasn't deterred by her comment
and he asked if she thought about joining the rodeo,

She said, "Hombre, I am a cultural czarina and prefer fast cars."
El gaucho rojo, was satisfied with her answers, then handed
her his card and stepped out to hail a cab, when she added,
"I'll be in Ft. Worth; I do hope to see you again."

Headed to Work

Como pendaja, you raced around the corner,
came fast as if being chased,
maybe your pendejo boyfriend distracted you,
made you carelessly do 40 on a left turn,
maybe it was practice for a Friday bank robbery
at 7:45 a.m. on this bright December morning.

I was headed 11 miles south
to teach my high school students,
waiting for the class door to fling open this cold day,
instead, I got my driver's-side headlight *smashed*,
I turned my anger into action, and I took
my own sharp turn to follow those two idiots.

They saw my blue Peugeot was behind them
then they took another sharp right turn,
but still managed to sideswipe and crash
three other cars before the chase ended.
Someone called 911, another victim shouted.

While the "speeders" scrambled to get out,
I stood at their driver's door,
holding a crow bar, I promised
I would use it on their ride
if they left —

They stayed seated until the cops showed up
and wrote them tickets, as to be expected,

11

they had no car insurance or driver's licenses
to show their lack of common sense.

I wanted restitution for the damage.
I said, "I'll drop the whole thing for 400 bucks."
The girl said, "Come on, follow us."
I drove behind them to Avondale to go speak to her mom.
When her mother saw me, she said, "What now, mija?"

I told her I could keep her daughter
out of getting a record and not report
the crash to my insurance or talk to a judge,
but her mom in a night robe,
with growing irritation in her eyes

stopped smoking that white mini-girder
tipping off the ledge of her fat lip,
exploded and screamed,
"TAKE HER DUMB ASS TO JAIL,
I don't give a damn! Maldita, she belongs there"

Oh, I realized, nothing is gonna change her mambo mama mind.
Outside, I asked the teen-gal's bowling-ball-novio Erasmo –
"Can you get me four hundred to makes this charge go away?
The repairs gonna take some green, ya feel me?"

Pushing past hesitation, he phones his primo
who shows up after 30 minutes in his Escalade,
hands pelón 20 twenties so the girlfriend
can get a real license—
someday—then again, maybe not.

Fronterizo Shopping Trip

In 1965, abuela's youngest son Tio Tony, aka Junior,
and his girlfriend Grace drove us across the Rio Grande
from the Texas border town of Eagle Pass to shop.
My primo Pino and I sat in rear seat,
and with us — unsmiling Grandma Jesusa.

All our skins branded brown by summer sun,
we sat mutely as the Border Patrol
waved us over, to ask, "Where are you all from?
Where you headed and
when are you coming back?"

Tio at the wheel, confident in his crew cut
and a smile as bright as his white tee shirt,
answered in command of Anglo-speak,
"Oh, we won't be long, just a quick
trip for a few baked goods."

His girlfriend teased him,
said he sounded like the gringo TV actor
on her favorite soap opera "Days of Our Lives."
Piedras Negras shopping was a quick
sweep down a thin street

Full of bargains of discounted crackers,
Bimbo bread, vanilla cookies,
coverless bundles of comics,
Mexican cokes & candies,
plus a new table cloth.

Uncle Tony bought a round container
of waxy pomade, La Parrot to "train his hair,"
between sips of his coke, he said,
"It beats Vaseline petroleum jelly
 and it smells better, too."

On the way back to Tio's sedan,
a skinny girl who followed us
holding a wrinkled bag called out,
"Se veden aguacates –
veinticinco centavos!"

Four ready-to-eat bumpy-skinned,
palm-size heft of tropical butter treats
all for just 25 cents!
Grandma gave her fifty cents,
two American quarters,

Which dashed my hopes of
buying brand-new comic books,
with her money,
instead, I could look at my
Tio's girlfriend's all-Spanish-language comics,

About a black school kid,
Memín Pinguin,
who wore a bright-striped tee shirt,
a baseball cap and a big smile
that rivaled Tio's.

Back at the border crossing gate, we slowed to a stop,
the driver's-side guard asked,
"Have anything to declare?
Any fresh fruits, vegetables, fresh cuts of meats?
Maybe a pet for the kids?"

A big-nose blond guy
on the car's other side scratched
his afternoon chin and said,
"What's in that paper bag, granny?"
He pointed with his fat fingers

At what Grandma cradled in her lap,
reached in the rolled down window
and snatched the dusty bag,
"What are these? –AH_VOCA_DoEs?!"
"Going have to keep these—you no take to Texas."

Disappointment seeped from my grandma's frown —
Tio apologized in his best English that his mother
doesn't think clearly,
she must have made that purchase
when he wasn't looking.

They just smirked,
and as if they were the Beatles,
said in unison "Yeah, yeah, yeah"—
and waved us to leave—

Abuela said, "Pinche rinches, como siempre,"
and pulled out a single hidden avocado from her apron,
peeled it and offered us each a bite,
but we didn't take a taste of warm green butter
instead, asked for cookies,

Tio said, "I don't want you kids to make a mess in my car."
Grandma replied, "You likey to drive? OK shut up!"
Primo Pino exclaimed, "Abuela, you can speak English!"
and the whole car laughed.

Stolen Blanket

I.

Criminally wrapped up in a dog-hair-covered blanket,
I didn't care who else froze –
Remember, if I were to tell you
I knew how to survive in the desert,
just walk the other way, that would be best, unless,
you too, were prepared to commit a crime.

Now even if you love dogs, would you want dog smell
and stray hairs covering your blanket?
If you say "yes," can you roll way over there?
Here's how the blanket became mine, I pulled it from
suburban lemon-yellow station wagon's half-opened window,
so much for my Catholic School training!

II.

We four dumb-asses drove from Chicago in an old sedan,
I didn't bring much, just my extra-firm toothbrush,
three Frito bags, a couple cans of corn & beans
and knowing we were going to the desert—
a few tee-shirts & six gallons of water.
(oralé, you thought I was gonna say cowboy hat!)

Trip organizer and driver Felipe "the Wolfman" Aguirre
brought menthol cigarettes, seven
packs of chewing gum, aviator sun glasses,
a map and his bed roll and mismatched socks.

I don't recall what the twin brothers Primo and Tivo
brought besides a case of bad breath Old-Style beer,
their dirty White Sox ball caps,
and hemorrhoid scowls.
Felipe did the daytime driving:
the twins drove after dark.
I was the "look out" guy.
Just us urban vatos scraggly
in mustaches and goatees,
with forehead bandanas

Searching for Arizona Aztlan in August
on an unemployed budget.
When we arrived at the Grand Canyon
getting almost towards sunset,
we unloaded on top of lumpy pine cones,
soon in the dark, summer's warmth disappeared, we tried to
fall asleep on top of newspapers
skid-row-style, used our balled-up jean jackets
as pillows —

at midnight, I stood up and stumbled away without a
flashlight until reaching the visitor's parking lot, seeking
warmth in the 55-degrees under the bug dancing glow of a
waxing moon

When I spotted my chance, yes, I stole
a tourist's vacationer blanket,
it was his dog's.
I did it soundlessly and with such stealth
it made me wonder if a disembodied Carrizo
scout were guiding me,
I had mystical mescaline night vision
to see it and later dreamt that same scout took
my only bandana, because
I woke up at dawn & it was missing.

Wearing the blanket like a serape,
with dust and dog hair stuck to me,
I grabbed the can opener, and opened
cans of pinto beans and sweet corn
to share with my traveling pals but
what they really wanted were
hot pancakes, pork sausages,
egg & papa tacos, fresh coffee
and conch-shaped pan dulce —

"What a bunch of dummies," I said, "Shut up.
Eat. There's food!" then they stiffly sat up
and made spoons out of stale corn chips,
in silence, we ate the cold-canned breakfast
plus, an occasional stray dog hair
or two for good measure.

Roseland Psychic

Black ice informs the road,
causing the evening drive to go slow,
then an unwanted prediction is made:
"We won't make it to the place, maybe,
we should just turn around."

The backseat teen psychic
who joined three adults in getting
high before heading
to a Dalton pre-Christmas party
had the vision.

Car skids to a stop
under a viaduct, why?
Rear tire pops, everyone out,
while it's changed, "And would
Geronimo, please shut up!"

The next day, psychic woke up
on the original weed-house couch,
he had dreamt the honest-to-Tim-Leary-
is-dead dream, and didn't know if he
made it to bardo state two or three.

It was a miserable Monday,
for the past 28 hours he had drifted
naked across jagged peaks

and valleys of an MDA–laced mind,
the glowing giddy glue of every touch was gone.

His merry hostess said good morning
from her sandalwood well-lit bedroom,
she felt like talking while her postman
was delivering out in the timid winter sun,
in zombie obedience, psychic

Went from the fold-out couch to her fluffy
cotton oasis where she let him rest his uncombed
head on her fleshy belly and breasts, where he slept
the sleep of an exile, seeking no words or wondering
was tenderly given bed-buddy duties instead.

Amish Hippies & City Slickers

At our B&B in Monteagle/Sewanee, Tennessee
we needed a simple metal vegetable steamer—
ya' know it looks like a noodle strainer,
only the holes are bigger,
so off we went to find one along the rural highway
with a population of 1,997 souls.

We drove for a bit, until we saw a place
that catered to natural food eaters,
an emporium with a little of everything –
refrigerated 50-dollar probiotics,
a thumb-size dried bundle of New Mexican sage
at ten dollars for smudging bathrooms,

They even had ghost-pepper salsa
and eight-dollar bags of blue corn chips,
but not a single veggie steamer!
We drove around and visited a few other places
until we saw what seemed to be the obvious joint –
a rainbow-colored sign announcing

"The Amish Hippie," and it was open!
Their front door was covered in Acid Rock iconography,
Jefferson Airplane, Quicksilver Messenger Service and Hendrix.
I went right for the main entrance, figuring
I looked grungy with a salt & pepper mustache,
a deep wine "University of the South"
tee-shirt and I had on my camouflaged baseball cap.

I proceeded to inquire in my best
Stephen Gaskin's Tennessee accent
if they sold veggie steamers,
"What's that?" asked the young rotund gal,
looking up from her video game.

My wife, with her thick Chicago accent, explained,
"Ya' know, it looks like a strainer, only da holes are larger,
and it folds open with metal pedals like a flower,
that's where da veggies go,
so, you put it at da bottom of a sauce pan
wit sum wawter."

The gal looked straight at me,
while I was standing next to my love,
and asked, "Wha' she just say?" as she put down
her video game's control console.
I did my best to repeat what had been said,
And when I finished the gal's male relative or friend

Stopped what he was doing,
packing and stacking tie-dyed tee-shirts,
and walked over to say, "Where y'all from?"
"Chicaawgo" she replied,
and they both grinned
and asked her to say it again.

At that point, it was clear they were funning with us,
but we remained calm and smiled.
Then the fellow said, "Did you check over

at Piggly Wiggly, across the road?"
I said, "Wouldn't you know it, we've already
been there hunting for that thing, but they didn't have it."

So, I thanked him and started for the door,
then the fellow called out, "Come on now ya'll,
take a look around before you head to
the Dusty Dollar Store or back to your Windy City."
We did a double take and felt a tad guilty about
not shopping at what seemed like a cool place,

Trying to stand out in the monotony
of all this green hilly country,
we examined their Rasta-colored back packs
and Bob Marley tee shirts and flags,
it all seemed so distant from Jamaica
with its reggae rhythms, jerked chicken.

Amid the kaleidoscope of colors
in the form of tie-dyed baby outfits,
some sparkling big bongs and plastic Frisbees,
piles of yarn-covered hacky sacks
gathered from the last Grateful Dead concert,
the hippie hereditary of yesterday all clearly
on display at this incense-smelling shop.

Then we spied some genuine hand-made
(Not from China) Cherokee medicine bags,
all stitched with sinew, light brown leather pieces
of pig suede, cow, or deer skin decorated with a

couple plastic barrel beads
on the closure cord,
I figured it would work for our hometown healer
friend to carry her shungite crystals or curative herbs,
like weed or dryer lint to make a fire, the medicine bag
even had a ball-point drawing of a dream catcher on it!

But we didn't see any cast-iron pots or pans,
wagon wheels or even horse shoes for sale,
just a bunch of modern things,

Not even a solitary Amish woman's bonnet
or Amish man's black
flat-brimmed hat for sale,
all we saw were just some young fat blond folks
playing video games and two disappointed
veggie-eating Chicagoans.

Mayans Over Montana

"There's more stars in the sky than hairs on a deer's pelt."
~ attributed to the Lacadon Mayan

1.

Before Chac, water & night sky lord
squeezes the clouds for rain, his old pals
two brothers, Ah Peku and Coyapa,
loud thunder makers, let all know it's coming.

Chac who smokes tobacco cigars outside heaven's house,
occasionally flicks ashes, seen as bright to pale meteorite
cinders sailing across mid-August skies; he does this
since his woman hates the smoke's pungent smell and ashes.

2.

The jungle's mightiest monkey climbs above the green
tropical canopy and asks, "Where does the sky end?"
The Mayan jungle answers, "Big mystery."
Monkey wonders if fireflies could flash so high.

Night sky lord and lady together keep balance below them,
in monkey's jungle, swarms of insects swirl around —
moon and manmade light, while starlight fades,
leaves sparkle evidence of their births or deaths.

3.
A trio of star-deprived monkeys from Chicago's cage

of blinding bright bulbs escapes and reaches rest under Montana's

darkest skies. They are rewarded by a munificent outshining

opulence of many-rumored constellations seen for the first time.

After Chac tires of casting teams of flickering cigar flashes,

a summer thunderstorm rolls in to cover the twinkling dark

jade sky with an atmospheric curtain & imperishable orchestra,

the thunder & rain makers: Ah Peku, Coyapa and Chac return again.

Your Old Felt Hat

So, you decided to show up
on that hot summer day in your
urban working man's blues and bandanna
topped off with that brim of sorrows and shade.

That old felt hat of yours—
a tiny bright parrot feather poking up
from the grey ribbon head band,
the hat's crown also dotted with Wobblies'

red flag and arched-back black cat union buttons,
ghostly Joe Hill's visage & departing words
"Don't Mourn! Organize!" and a nod to
your Internationalist sympathies with bold

Spain's Anarcho-Syndicalist CNT flag
along your border of brown stale sweat & salt,
the same hat that makes your wife wince
and wished aloud before she left,

"Karloki, get rid of that,
please toss it in the trash,
por favor, don't leave that scata hat &
on top the dinner table, you donkey!"

Hours you waited at Chicago's O'Hare International gates
— standing, sitting, standing and staring at the tarmac for
that flight across the Atlantic to land with your smiling
wife that was away a whole summer season in Greece.

She appears and you shout "Mariana!" your arms go up at
45 degrees, ready to embrace –all that you missed
she hugs you blissfully and kisses lips beneath mustache,
unconcerned with that old felt hat above your face.

Bricks Revisited

apologies to Robert Nighthawk, and AWOL Roy Collier, US Army

Got bricks in my pillow
wheel gun beside my bed,
I've got bricks in my pillow
can't seem to rest my head,
these nights I can't sleep,
who is coming to my door?

My tub is filled with treasure,
ain't selling ditch weed no more,
I finally have some money,
just can't take a bath,
always worried 'bout somebody
gonna take my stash.

There're nights I hear moths flappin'
cross the ceiling above my bed,
yeah, I also hear spiders crawlin'
whispering songs about the dead,
I've got lead in my water,
I've got mud in my ice cubes too,

I've got moon honey in my tea,
might go to Texas soon,
I've got grounds in my coffee,
big black dog by my door
I've got grounds in my coffee,
don't know what I'll do anymore.

30

They've taken my shoes laces,
and mailed them to a whore.
I've got holes in my pockets,
books of matches are what I read,
landlord wants the past two months
I better go sell me some seeds.

Got bricks in my pillow
wheel gun beside my bed, but
just can't seem to rest my head,
I feel it's time for leavin',
but I don't know where to go,
guess it's time to pack a duffle bag,
get away from crazy Chicago.

Caw Caw Caw

Summer's vacant phone wires strung across
this once crow friendly alley, no crows for weeks
since the West Nile virus arrived
on needle swarms of inky mosquitoes.

Common crow cacophonies would entertain me
but these murders of crows faded away
and in less time than it took to say,
Cleopatra loved Marc Anthony.

Who else misses' crows, their shapes and sizes?
Let me drive around with my truck windows down
and listen, wait, oyes, Caw, caw, cawwww!
I blow my horn and imitate their call-in conjunction.

What sprouts up in my dream-bearing mente
is that I'll have time to scrape ice and shovel
lots of snow before the crows ever hatch
and come back to the city.

Inside my kitchen, I pour a cup of coffee,
it's bitter Bustelo and black as crow's feathers,
si muy amargo sin azúcar y leche, I drink it
without the few ingredients to turn it sweeter.

I sip, and watch the skies and empty telephone
wires, waiting for new spring crows returning—
then two appear and perch side to side,
Bienvenido, winged corvus corax a tú Chicago.

Obama in Mexico

Once Obama flew to Mexico's
Districto Federal, the nation's heart
he marveled at the frantic opera of 20 million
eating while going deaf *Chilangos*.

He, toured the grand museum with a Mexican man,
who died, the very next day from a virus — H1 N1— swine flu.
What were chances of that happening?

One, two, buckle my shoe, *three, four* — close the door,
five, six — pickup sticks, all they did was bump fists after
#44 Prez took notes from the soon-to-be-dead man who explained
Teotihuacan prophecy to the guests.

seven, eight, lay them straight,
both men stood in the shadow of ancient
(Cuahtli eagle + caxitl bowl)

Nine, ten, don't risk it again,
when "Caledario Azteca" is 12 feet in diameter,
25 tons of hand-carved glyphs and symbols,
remains a mystery even to presidents—
and maybe to you and
maybe for me.

Snovember Travels

50 days before Covid-19

As the plane's cone bottom tip burst through white tigers
and dragon-shaped clouds that for five hours surrounded us—
I wanted feet on the Icelandic beach
or in the Blue Lagoon again.

Once on the ground, just above us,
not one, but two suns!
Just a tongue in the sky made of rain and curiosity
formed over the shores of cold Lake Michigan.

We traveled far and it offered me
a chance to become a stoic meteorologist
with what truth I saw in trance after you asked,
what was coming?

I gestured with hands rolling over and over.
"Confusion, everything upside down," I said,
"Eventually the thorns of missed opportunities
will leave from the soles of our feet,

"While the sun's golden-pollen-arrowhead
will rise again at the edge of an inland sea
behind eyelashes that blink on the brink
after months of masks."

ALMOST INVISIBLE TALENTS

On the King's Road in San Antonio, Tejas

for César A. Martinez

Humble householder, modern-Tejano Toltec
welcomes us to his armadillo-corrugated casa
while he opens his guarded black-clippings binder.

It reveals a parade of rostros de los Chicanos muertos
and others posed in their favorite or final public photos,
we ponder once-alive, many-ceased orbits,

notice how heat has oxidized white print--to brown.
he draws and paints as deliberate as science allows,
forms prisms from the heart crystal,

Out of each human face,
resurrection springs in new colors
inside the artist's mind studio, a magician's

Mortuary, without mourners' tears
or egocentric memories,
decades gone grins, sunglasses,

squints and sampaku stares live again,
afloat on the tapestry of luxuriant
magentas, greens and umbers.

César's magic a peyote kaleidoscope
snapped open, towers of firecrackers
sizzle in a torrent of canvas strokes.

While listening to silver chords of España's
flamenco which accompanies him
as he strikes and strums one magnetic brush,

flashing side to side, open/closed,
like el toreador's dance to free
the bull of blindness with shafts of light.

Leap Year

for E. Donald Two-Rivers
06/29/1945-12/28/2009

Coming back from your tool-and-die job you realized
you had something better to offer than near exhaustion,
you rode slumped on that bus near California and Archer
when a friendly freckle-faced gal lugged
her college book bag aboard and sat next to you.

"She was one sexy prairie chicken,
in a Midwestern sort of way," you said on the phone
the next day, telling me how you might have showed her
Uptown right off the Lawrence "El"
where it's always good times for hillbilly and Indian drinking.

You told her about your book coming out
—*A Dozen Cold Ones,*
on your "February 29, leap-year birthday,"
she wanted to see a poem, so, you thumbed through
your greasy notebook and pulled out an unfinished piece.

She started to read when she suddenly
yanked on the grey cord
and got off pocketing your poem,
but you had not exchanged names,
just smiles and a wave goodbye.

Maybe you knew this was going to happen, all psychic-like
after your Truman college Red Path performance
when James Yellowbank stood on top of a Wilson Avenue snow drift
after a night of cigarette singing, still pissed off to go panhandle
for his liquid addiction which caused him to gamble

His health like a Ho Chunk casino patron,
you said, "Damn, I'm going to miss him,"
maybe it was then you decided to change your residence
and wife, or was it the other way around as
we returned from an all-Indian poetry reading

going west on multilingual-Montrose
that you saw doe-eyed Beverly on the sidewalk
sauntering in boots and tight jeans.
You declared, "Buddy, in a month that
pretty gal is gonna' go out with me."

"Do you know her?" I asked, and you replied,
"Sort of, but I know you don't believe me —
ya think I'm way too old and she's so fine."
"But watch me, bro, just watch me."
"Yeah, Eddy," I said, "I'll be watching."

Canto of Heaven/Tlalocan or Hell/Mictlan —

for Ricardo
(3/29/1941-9/3/1995)

Can Chicanos lay claim to our own Homer, Milton or Baudelaire?
Pues wáchele, what are we to think cuando Ricardo Sánchez,
El Poeta Highly Developed, our Ph.D. in more than barriology,
linked to those immortals by master scholar Felipe de Ortego y Gasca
in the forward of pioneering *Canto y Grito mi Liberación.*

I first read Sánchez during the anchor 70s, as he explored in masterful
code-switching Spanish and English the American devil's bargain of his life,
after Soledad prison pains was he really like the cover's painting
of young sunburnt mustache chuco in cool hat, unflinching stare of sly guy
with reefer-cooked eyes & totally fed up with bogus borders,

Con tattoos hidden under a ruddy camisa's turned-up collar?
He was fully aware his turbulent years were not over,
especially when he declared—
"We shall create our own Chicano society y si no le gusta al gringo..."
OR *"Will the future disinter our bones and sing praises to*
 Chicanosaurian poetics
in some distant mausoleum of diversity?
Whatever our destiny it will be something
that we will have created through the pain of daring
to be ourselves at whatever cost."

I met him first in San Antonio, at Floricanto, later we all joined others –
los Southwest and Midwest cultural activists to create Cantos al Pueblo
con indio-xicano-artists in murals, music, and poetic narratives en Milwaukee,
Corpus Christi, St. Paul, Phoenix, Carbondale, and lastly Chicago—
I lament millions of people had not heard his cantos o liberating llantos,

41

Nor ever read a word of Ricardo's hefty *Hechizospells*
nor slim *Milhuas Blues and Gritos Norteños,*
fortunately, we still have his many fine libros ready to be mined
of their potent poetic ore, for he offered us his rage & love—
real human treasure, maybe, that's all a poet can do
before they go towards tlalocan or mictlan forever.

It is dream

for Jeff Abby Maldonado

We emerged from the dark charcoal blanket of night,
our ancestors foraged for more than food,
they generated the genius seed of all Toltecs.
It is too big for hooks, spears, arrows or nets.

It is dream.
You watch for its presence with hunter-gatherer eyes and heart,
it climbs and descends,
offering a compass to fertile gardens, as we walked the land.

Tiny hummingbird heads south—
alights on the breeze where Huitzilopochtli
directed the first Mexicas to nectar
savored in crimson beaks and ruby tongues—

Come, return to us again in art.
It is dream.
You are the young guardian of grand designs,
son of the codex's keepers, mound magicians and pyramid musicians.

Sure-footed and agile as the spider-web mathematician,
within a spinning galaxy of delta paints,
you dive unburdened into the healing fires
to retrieve what's hidden inside the obsidian mirror.

Hobo Skills

for Koyokuikatl

My friend, El Viejo, called it "free food,"
he rose early to harvest it at sidewalks' edge,
or in neighbor's yard by brass faucet.

He found plump green rhizomic exclamation point clusters,
soft-skinned in spring, its chlorophyll flame
penetrates taste bud and brain,

Comes close to lemon watercress,
offers a bit of mental clarity for the curious.
"Be alert to its tricky twin," the old man warned,

"Careful with impersonator Hairy-Stemmed Spurge,"
he added, "What's edible is duckweed, portulaca,
verdolagas, 'free food,' because it is all wild purslane."

"Viejo, how did you find all this out?"
He replied, "My father during the Great Depression
learned from an old hobo, good at finding free food."

Autumn Equinox

for David Pesqueira

Wooden hatchet's handle
smooth from use across 20 years,
its steady blade bites an edge off.

Hard-dried logs surrender inner secrets,
reveal striated furrows,
growth changes in uneven pieces,

To become tinder when tossed on embers
sacrificed for insurgent orange-flame dance,
once again you share, "Aho, my relatives."

We greet season's first sun-rise
on this windy shore, copal & sage
smoke red Čhaŋnúŋpa in our circle
with prayers of remembered rituals.

O'José, Can You See?

¿Me oyes? ¿Qué hacer? ¿Mañana, qué hacer?
No hay un cielo mexicano,
solo un infierno americano
y el pinche "Popo*" always
looking to bury the grand city
that's sinking.

Got it? What to do? Tomorrow, what to do?
There's no Mexican heaven, only an American
hell, and damn "Popo" siempre queriendo
enterrar la gran ciudad que se está hundiendo.

~ *Popocatepetl is an active volcano near Mexico City*

46

Singing Chihuahua

Childless Southside Roseland relatives,
Tia Francis & Tio Frank,
loved to play accordion,
even taught favorite chihuahua
Pepito to sing.

During a visit they played us
a tipsy tune, Pepito el perrito,
watched in the front room
with quizzical big dark eyes,
now up on hind legs

Bouncing to red and
ivory notes of Tio's
polka box from Carrizo Springs.
Tio & Tia insisted it was time
"Cantale Pepito cantale!"

He howled over and over while
my mom and I joined in
with our own bouncy
ding gaga ding, a ding,
a ding a ding, gaga ding!"

Nuestra Dia Con Doña Jesusa

Backyard of faded and broken
weather-beaten wooden pickets
decades old, bound by rusty wire
corrals us loud grandkids,
like pollitos at her side.

At the yard's edge rows of beaver-tailed nopales
host ripe sweet red and purple fuzzy needle fruit
that Doña Jesusa collects with knife,
fork and bowl in early morning dew
along with a few pomegranates.

Dawn's cool ground as yet to heat when los gallos
start their greetings across the village roads and sky.
Dona's chores this morning include soaking laundry,
as we play tag, our footprints are erased beneath
an unexpected brief sun shower.

Rain drops popping puffs of tiny dust volcanoes,
releasing earth perfume,
minerals, mesquite and cactus flowers,
come afternoon, summer's harsh sun is momentarily
blocked by a passing gang of lumbering clouds

Offering spotty shade to us kids
and potted plants growing
strong in a mixture of pebbles, clay and soft sand.

Abuela suggests we'll round up fireflies—
luciérnagas, after the sun goes down,

We will catch some and seal them up
inside old glass jars,
but must promise
to set them free
before we go to sleep.

The Circus

A cougar's howl blasts out of brass cornets,
matched by blaring bugles,
thunderous trombones,
plus, two marching kettledrums
dum, dum, dumbing us deaf,
as six muscle men carry cudgels,
four women wearing less than
what's wrapped in ribbon around their lances
bounce freely alongside 13 elephants
that line up, turn, mount
and massage each other,
except grey guys one and thirteen
who represent wrinkled Alpha and Omega
cosmic pachyderms possessing
the patois of saints
amid the frantic pulse of these
under-the-big-top idiotics.

Late October's

city darkness under a canopy
of bending shapes moved by lake breezes,
allowing lonely street lamp lights to silhouette
rusted leaves and branches

To create a changing camouflage,
while dropping last season's
stragglers that collect on wet ground
near the walled-in cemetery.

Quietly, with deliberate steps,
I move across a sidewalk, where once
a Potawatomi Indian trail ran
northwest to southeast.

Patches of decades old cobblestone
are revealed where asphalt
has worn away,
on a street used every day.

Standing next to the green
and gray pipe of a bus stop,
one bright bus and its bread-box face
from nearly a quarter mile away approaches,

I've changed my mind, decided
not to board, yet fully expecting it to stop,
I turned myself invisible—
the bus driver doesn't slow

Or acknowledge my presence,
and continues to go...
invisibility abilities please me;
I knew right then I'd have a choice

For Halloween,
to become dark shadow man
or a bus stop without a sign.

Our Circle's Song

relies on full-lung power,
sung as beach sand covers our feet,
we lean split logs into a small pyramid,
set it on fire, its trail of smoke
rises to greet the coming sunlight.

This is what we do when winds
bring in seasonal change to expand
or contract our circle's participants—
we draw closer especially in
below-freezing temperatures.

But on this dawn, dozens join in
for autumnal equinox transformation,
the gathered offer prayers for all,
for those slowly losing sight,
or engaged in the fight for clean water.

"Mni Wiconi, Water is Life!"
wisdom of the ages—
we offer praise
and health & help
for all the relations.

We salute newlyweds and the old,
couples with three daughters or sons,
that also join us here at the shore line,
some friends' footprints have faded,
but they are still remembered,

Healers and wounded, students and teachers,
have become singers who know the prairie songs,
wide-open-sky songs, welcoming-new-life songs,
we are all remnants of the upheaval, in Turtle Island's
post-colonial indigenous affirmation.

Our circle includes visitors from all four Directions—
Asia minor, major and Africa's interior, US southern Carrizo,
Central American Spanish speakers, Middle Easterner Muslim,
Irish, Jewish and Canadian Cree, Great Lakes Ojibwa Anishinaabe
and curious dog-loving tourists from the suburbs—taking a "selfie,"

Mexican Nahuatl-speakers who offer copal and embrace
Arizona Yaquis, New Mexican Laguna Pueblo brother
serves as protector for the American Indian Center's
eagle staff feathers as Choctaws handle the drums,
the circle's heart resides with David Tlateollin,

In pre-dawn fog duties, he shapes an altar
upon the sand and gently places
sage bundles cleared from the shadows
of the Black Hills, out of a carved wooden box a
sacred chanunpa is unwrapped from its deer's skin bundle.

Smooth blood-red stone and willow stem-free
from blemish is slowly packed with ritual tobacco,
David took this task to heart and pledged before
the sacrificial tree to remember Sun Dance teachings,
to honor his teacher Selo Black Crow, pipe carrier.

Calm Panic

for JXC

You offer us sonic bread, composed of well-
kneaded beats, turn spirals out of triangles,
electric audio dominance soars, calls up
boisterous ghosts set to dancing.

Muscle memories bring fingertip callouses
where talent rules—releases a roaring Niagara Falls
where we drown in your opus sound playground,
eyes on you as you levitate the room,

Take us for a wild ride down Bryn Mawr,
reveal a youthful grace across your face,
smiles spring from the still combing, going bald
and Q-tip heads which bob to your rhythmic rolling.

All drunk-on note-symmetry-winged dreams
sailing across the ceiling, no one can see the walls anymore –
prisoners to your cinematic hailstorm
volcanic eruption– snow storm—wind shear—tornado blowing

Decibels of delight in the fresh-breeze bliss
that beckons amid fading summer light,
asymmetrical danger leaps out at us
like from a deep shadowy favela,

On the outside, windshields crack at the high note,
piercing drum percussion without warning, all soar
above eagles and satellites, after your inner keyboard
pilot nods permission for lift off in savage illumination!

Homage: He Didn't Stop Singing

July 16, 1948 – May 27, 2021

Last night I dreamt que nuestro amigo
Jesús Chuy Negrete shared corridos con
Mexico's heroes Villa y Zapata,
they applauded, called him maestro
compañero Chicano –

It is true, que Jesús remembered
their sacrifice for justice,
honored them and their soldiers,
humble people de la tierra
that lacked a home and fair wages.

For harsh is the hand and heart
of los ricos and imperialists –
Jesús was a man who took a stand,
singing, "Which Side Are You On?"

Nuestro Chuy, our musical historian,
recounted many deeds across five centuries,
los cinco siglos cuando los españoles reached
las playas de Veracruz before Tenochtitlan
carrying a plague for gold y plata,
to feed priests, pimps and royal poverty.

Negrete revealed to you and me Mexican struggles
from the sixteenth to twentieth centuries,
was it sparked after being inspired by
Denver's Crusade for Justice founder
Rodolfo "Corky" Gonzales?

Chuy admired "Corky's" famous
epic poem Yo Soy Joaquín,
which Jesús would frequently recite
with some slight alterations –

"I am Cuauhtémoc, proud and noble-King of an empire,
civilized beyond the dreams of the Gachupín Cortés,
who is also the blood, the image of myself –
I am Nezahualcoyotl,
first poet warrior Hungry Coyote,
I am the sword and flame of Cortés
the despot, and I am the cuauhtli eagle
and coatl serpent of the Mexica"

Chuy met con César Chávez y Dolores Huerta
as they were building an organization,
a union for all doing back-breaking
agricultural labor to feed millions.
Chuy made common cause
with the Midwest's FLOC and
Texas Farm Workers Union, too.

He sang of his Southeast side family,
families of Pilsen y La Villita, he sang
of prisons y barrio school room challenges
where the system changed our names
or gave us grief for being in the parks
or the streets with or without "papeles."

His canciones were heard in Havana, Cuba,
to the cheers of an international audience,
a week later, he sang in a friend's backyard,

he was known from San Francisco to Boston,
was a frequent guest in Houston, Dallas,
San Antonio and Austin. He was known in
Whitewater, Wisconsin, Gary, Indiana,
Iowa City and Muscatine, too.

He devoted years learning Spanish and English
folkloric ballads and legendary lyrics,
he treasured the works of Victor Jara, Gabino Palomares,
Utah Philips, Amparo Ochoa, Bob Dylan, Joe Hill and Woody Guthrie—
Occasionally, he joked around with one hit wonders by Johnny Horton,
a gringo balladeer singing his *The Battle of New Orleans*—

But Chuy being serious, we recall his take on Carlos Puebla's
"Aquí se queda la clara
la entrañable transparencia
de tú querida presencia
COMANDANTE Ché GUEVARA"

Pués Chuy, he knew a thousand cultural workers
of every color and culture, his closest were Chicanos:
muralistas, teatro actors, dancers & players,
poetas, painters, puppeteers and sculptors.

He knew los Southsiders now gone: Benny Ordoñez,
los brothers, Vicente & Francisco Mendoza, he knew
Casa Aztlan's Moth Barrera & Martín Cabrera, fiery Magda Ramirez,
he knew March member Marguerite Ortega, he knew muralist José Guerrero,
he knew talented María Salcedo, Hector Gamboa, Rey Vasquez and
Salima Rivera, he knew Colorado's activist poet Lalo Delgado,

Who taught him, *if George Washington was my father,*
why wasn't he Chicano–
y los first Brown Berets, y pinto poets todos de Tejas,
Raúl Salinas, Ricardo Sánchez y Tigre Perez
Tambien like you and me he was friends con El Viejo,
Carlos Cortez, Chicago's printmaker poet Koyokuikatl.

In search of classic corridos Chicanos y Mexicanos,
Jesús came to know los Alacranes Mojados con
el Chunky Sánchez y tambien los hermanos,
Daniel y Luis Valdez de Teatro Campesino.

It's clear Jesús heard los cantos
al sexto sol traveling America's
barrios y borderlands, under smokestacks
and skyscrapers, he sang for those who punched
the clock and walked the picket line,

He sang with his four sisters Martha,
Juanita, Santa and Rosa,
parents, nieces and nephews,
he sang with his wife Rita &
sons Joaquín & Lucas
he also gave voice to los cholos & locos,
the exiled and guys returning wounded
from war, while suffering alongside our
next generation of students--the Dreamers.

It wasn't easy to get Chuy to sit still, but
once we walked from his parent's place

for afternoon coffee and pan dulce
at a greasy spoon on Commercial Street.

In the booth he confided to me,
"Ese loco, what do you think it would take
 to get on pinche Saturday Night Live?"
I replied, "I don't know, do you
want to be on television?"

"Yeah, Cumpián — I would love to perform
dressed como El Johnny Cash all in black,
wearing shades, I might sing
'Brown-eyed Children of The Sun'
 y algo en español,

"I bet some might confuse me
with José Feliciano, but that's cool, too,
I could end my set with a love song,
a boléro, behind me a chorus of beautiful
black women as my back up,
hallelujah-like angels,
that would blow minds.

"Oralé carnal—
I need to get back to la casa
and make some calls,
I have to get ready because
I'm going on a NEW TOUR."

HEROICS AND MYSTERY CULTS

1963

Even the concrete lawn ornament "Black Jockey,"
rebelled and broke rank beneath the restaurant's
big red Coca-Cola sign and joined up with
the truck drivers, maids, janitors and field hands
rudely being jostled and beaten by Birmingham's
armed uniformed white cops barking orders
along with two German shepherds in their trained
frontline mercenary roles tearing at one
young man's good Sunday sweater, over and over.

Slow Going

Standing behind my wooden teacher's desk,
pen in hand, I scan the room and the roster
of my new September's sophomore division,
I see some lost freshmen are here, too.

Taz Williams appears as the loud period bell burns our ears,
Taz normally moved like an unencumbered Ninja,
but this morning he seemed to have a stone in his shoe.
After aroll call I asked if he'd take the mandatory
count to the attendance office.

He said, "Ok, but it's gonna be slow going."
"Hey, what happened to you? I asked.
He said, "Let me show you Cumpián."
He rolled his loose pants up to his knee and stopped,
pointed to a dark bruise indentation on the side of his calf.

"Caught a stray bullet, smaller caliber, maybe 22 ammo.
Damn, it took me by surprise, I was nearly at my crib's door
when some fool fired from a van's window, I got inside and hit the floor.
My grandma called 911, I bled, but nothing major—just ruined her nice rug.
I won't go out after midnight no more, too many gangsters
doing their purge thing."

This is the sort of "What I did on My Summer Vacation" account that
no student should have to write about.
I said, "Taz, I'm glad you survived summer break,
take your time going to the office and getting back."

64

Century Twenty Malachi

"But Esau I hated, and made his mountains a desolation,
and gave his heritage to the jackals of the wilderness." — *Malachi 1:3*

Inter-office robot brought snail-mail across Sears & Roebuck's
26th floor rolling cubicle to cubicle,
beeping to alert us
there's more charts and memos
from the on-high command.

We trusted his sound, our aeneous mechanical messenger
in the march of marketing merchandise,
his wheels paid for by our innovative Elohim
who issued serious letters with help of secretary angels
and their spinning IBM Selectric alphabet balls

As demi-god Xerox made copies and filled us
with what was just about to be forgotten,
retail goals, profit forecasts,
we the dauntless dozen plotted against local
Esau brothers: Woolworths & Penney's,

Whose nickel and dime machinations built
friendly suburban malls
and State Street's desolation,
O' Robot Malachi, named for an Old Testament prophet—
that never saw the light-blue blinking eyes of modernity,

Rubber-wheeled, battery-operated
grey employee

making those 30-second pit stops,

you brought us our Bible -- in 1978, the Sears' catalog,

for it was a sacred tradition, we had none better before us.

We begged them not to

toss you out in 1980, Malachi,

onto that mountain of planned obsolescence,

like some workers, bow-legged and beaten

from lugging and sorting.

You saved me from a spider's bite

"See him crawling on the wall,
he is black and very small,
Boris the spider" ~ The Who

A lone eight-legged ninja slid down its silver string,

in preparation to strike. Two-fang punctures and a swipe.

Have you ever been bit? Do I look like a fly to a spider's eyes?

Suddenly you came over, observant amiga,

with your uncluttered vision and calm voice,

"There's a spider right above your shoulder."

Your words saved me from another dose of venom,

I would have been another unsuspecting victim

of that corner-lurking creep, whose eight-legged relative

Just two years earlier at the same spot,

reached my nape, cut me deep,

making a two-holed itchy lump that hurt for weeks.

With Only Smoke to Cover Me

Tobacco shag clings onto rough, dry lips as I moisten
a hand-rolled cigarette with tongue tip, resting,
half-naked on county's concrete floor, save for
a few sheets of rolling paper to cover me.

From ankles to knees, I've turn sandy
across bound-shackled muscles
that have carried me to this bony cell,
where there's nothing to do, except smoke.

I wait for my day before the judge's robe and rules,
and freeze at forty-eight degrees,
it started before Christmas, when guilt flushed through me
feeling fresh-from-the-sweat-lodge mind.

That's when I was arrested as I returned that thick
bright wool Pendleton blanket,
"borrowed" from the Anglo's fancy gift shop,
selling relics & dream catchers

Made by a bogus Chief Rollin-Dice-in-the-Casino tribe,
and their 19th Century settler nostalgia museum,
just what was I thinking, *kola, mi amigo,*
that praying "All My Relations, *o'mitakuye oyasin"*
would protect my flat nalgas, until
I was able to shamble clear out of town?

Just find the door

If your bed shakes as the closet doors swing open
at 4:13 in the darkest of mornings, you sit up to see
who is bouncing on the floor, then a swelling series
of car alarms reach you from cracked windows.

Now there's vibrations—and more—shockwaves,
that send you out in underwear and socks,
like your neighbors, you run outside
to see what's left of the block.

A wall of vehicles knocked over,
the wail of car and smoke alarms rile the air,
as eyes widen to homes that have been flattened
under piles of boards and brick.

At least your feet are covered amid the crunch of plaster and glass,
the air crackles with cries for help as others appear on the sidewalk,
flushed out of blankets and beds, leaving purses, cellphones,
handguns and dusty gym bags behind.

Morning overloads with howls and shouts for a medic,
soon a half-filled plastic water jug appears out
of a neighbor's open hand, its kindly shared just a sip
mitigates cotton mouth and the metallic taste of fear.

Haiti *(2010)*

A teenage girl was rescued alive from under a house in Port-au-Prince yesterday, 15 days after the devastating earthquake that killed as many as 200,000 people. Darlene Etienne, believed to be 16 or 17, was dehydrated and had a broken left leg but was conscious when she was dragged out of the rubble by rescuers. A rescue worker, JP Malaganne, described her as happy, shocked and crying. ~ The Guardian News Service

January sun presses down,
amplifies tropical heat lit inside
fluorescent chipped lime walls of the
crowded stale classroom.

It's a task to read my raggedy text book,
fabric threads unglued,
its old spine slowly peels away from the
book's brown-pages, bone dry at the edges.

To keep flies and mosquitos out,
most of the school's windows were painted shut,
but I could still hear from a courtyard away,
beyond thin glass, so much commotion.

An angry chorus of 200 political science students
with hands clapping like hammers smashing against bricks
echoes in protest against the university's mistreatment of a professor,
who lectured about Haiti's generational *"La corruption."*

It's nearly dinner, I can't wait to get home to eat,
I hope Pascal offers me a ride on his motorcycle,
plus, he really knows some short cuts
in and out of central Port-au-Prince.

I'm glad mama's making fish and rice tonight,
my lunch was two bananas and tea,
that's all I brought in my mad dash
to catch the Metro bus.

Pascal just returned my call, imagine we met three
weeks ago, in science class—environmental ecology,
maybe by bonne Saint Valentin's day,
we'll be more than study-circle friends.

Then, to my left, the floor shook, it went dark,
 I lost my seat as the ceiling started to crumble,
we all placed books and hands over our heads
as we were jolted side to side.

After it caved in, cracked glass, beams and brick blocks
buried us in a shower of shards, pipes and screams,
it's been over a day since I've lain here, my book still in hand,
feeling its stringy spine binding as I slide my free fingers.

My other arm is pinned under my aching hip,
I lay in this triangle of life while I slip in and out
of sleep across what feels like five days,
I tell time by a sliver of light that lasts a few hours.

Then it's more numb darkness,
I hardly can speak, my tongue dried as dust,
no one replied when I asked if someone could hear me?
Didn't I say that an hour ago? Or was it two days?

I have dust in my hair, ears and teeth,
someone for the Love of Jesus get this room off me,
this is a university; they must know we're still here…
I don't really know how to pray it seems.

God, please I'll gladly trade my university degree
for water and fresh air—He must have heard me as
I dreamt my mother saying, "Darlene Etienne, please
wake," as her tears touched my bruised face.

Most Won't Have Krishnamurti's Crown

Once you hit 50 and your hairbrush
still has its original purpose, you're one lucky S.O.B.,
you might say you won the genetic lottery,

So stop the wig commercials, it's crazy to believe
in onion juice cures rubbed on the scalp
will make you delicious with curls, plus you'll smell.

Maybe there's no laser savior, special space light
technology to grow hair back in the twenty-first century;
all you'll need are deep pockets, a heaven for credit card wishe$,

So go online, or phone to seek victory over
the receding Neanderthal nest that some
Sasquatch Bigfoot might show you how to maintain,

That modern comb dome covered with protein shafts,
as the civilized bastards hoist their stadium
of baseball caps while howling with indignation.

I do my working out in a GRUNGE GYM

Where there's NO air conditioning – just seven ceiling fans,
and only five ever spin – so shower before you come in,
if you wash your hands, it's a mechanic's slop sink located
inside a closet, next to eight tiny lockers big as shoe boxes,
which accommodate next to nothing.

There's free parking across a busy street,
where gangsters keep watch on you
from their apartments,
so maybe your car might lose a tire,
get towed, if you decide to get back late.

Steady sweating gals and guys thud-smash large free weights,
doing it before four picture windows with burning florescence.
No gawkers stop to smear the glass for fear of brutes inside,
there's no drinking fountain, you should have brought ya own H_2O,
ignore the wall clock, it's broken like the handle above the toilet hole.

The nice thing is when you enter no one
acknowledges your presence – unless grunts count,
everyone is too busy doing sit ups and 50-pound kettlebell squats –
if you're ever bothered by too much moisture in your area,
the manager will offer you some Windex and a rag.

Some nights, the air is an assortment of international male jock funk:
Africans straight from Ghana, Mexicans from towns missing men,
Filipinos from one of a hundred listless islands,
third-gen Chicagoans, newly tattooed farm boys
and highlanders from Poland and Ukraine.

The desk guy is named Dakota.
I wondered if he's native.
(He sorta looks it), got thick dark straight hair
and almond-tip eyes. He says, Japanese and Irish,
and speaks better than a public radio reporter.

Occasionally he'll write an encouraging message on the wall
in chalk as his blonde girlfriend does 200-pound dead lifts,
"Don't be disappointed with the results you've got, just think
of the work you didn't do today & stop looking at my lady–Foo!"

Company Manners

Steamier than a night watchman's chair cushion in Alabama,
hotter than a Mexican woman meteorologist on Spanish TV,
we're here in new tropical Chicago – you got that overburdened-
coat-rack-in-January look – but you should be smiling – it's July.

There's hot and cold coffee, stale and fresh flavors in the shape of
doughnuts and bagels – we have a bowl of Gaba Calm dopamine
receptors available in lemon and orange, and chair yoga from 7:45 to 8:15
in the employee lounge; yes, the same one under construction for years.

Nearing 94 in the Loop, honking cars and crowded concrete,
we make the one p.m. dash for super-caffeine sugar-laden lunches,
walking as fast as legally permissible, moving like boneless squids
across the wireless landscape making no eye contact under dark glasses.

We have slave-status silk ties up to the Adam's apple,
collars starch snug and top buttoned – long sleeves rolled all
the way to our flexible metal or cow leather-banded sweat-soaked
watches that peek out under cuff fabric.

We agree any guy removing his blue blazer
or khaki-colored sport coat pays for lunch.

Returning to the central-air rehydrating coolness of capitalism
at it's fashionable best, I wash my hands and dry them in contrast
to the spongy moistness of my cotton socks. I ask myself,
who else does masochistic games like me and these guys I work with?

They Buried Him at Sea

After they found Biggie and Tupac's
bullet-ventilated SUVs,
all crashed making a million-dollars-worth of debris,
scattered under cactus and skinny Joshua trees,

They canceled the video about
first rappers on the moon,
which won't be coming out too soon, because one LA
weed-smoker, insulted a prime-time diamond egoist

Calling him the voice of one big Ground Zero,
which reminds me, how did unlucky building number seven
implode on camera, as if on cue,
with no Jihadist or wreaking crew?

The planes hit from well over a block away of the World Trade
Twin Towers on that not so gentle Tuesday—
that had to be a false flag,
because only war hawks and oil men saluted.

Now chumps can argue back and forth as to how it happened,
the same way some argue that Tupac ain't dead,
or how nobody knows who kills so-called famous rappers or why —
"Damn says a six-grader, "it musta be the Illuminati!"

Can anyone tell me what became of
that tall bearded man
aboard the U.S. Navy ship, that was
bleeding through his white turban?

So why?

So why can't get along better?
I asked my father who had been a soldier
and worked as a migrant crop picker, he said,
"Humans made the wrong choice in leaving
hunting and gathering traditions, ever since we
started settling down to one piece of ground
to grow crops, raise livestock in large numbers,
& took steps to be 'fruitful and multiply,' seeking
ways to one up neighboring tribes for resources."

Damage was done by those who feared the wind,
they laid down more cement, called it a project,
but not beautiful,
they flayed the boreal woodland and tropical forests,
dug deep coal and heated their cities with its measure,
called it necessary and sold it.

They refused to sleep under nighttime suns and
made their own pitiful mercury light bulbs,
they set up artificial turf, dyed soccer fields green,
there's plastics in the fish we (can't) eat
as water pours out from a latrine.

They encased whole areas under the equator coveting last
best parts of deep jungle selva (salvation) in Brazil, Bolivia,
Colombia, Ecuador, Guyana, French Guiana,
Peru, Suriname and Venezuela for unrenewable
deforestation, first slowly, then suddenly,

whole skies ossify to metallic white,
now we can't see the daytime moon
—*is there a way we can turn back?*

Deforestation brings mercenaries to hunt down two-legged guardians
of 8.4 million square kilometers or 3.2 million square miles –
they look for the soft targets among 500 tribal groupings
those who make pleas in Spanish & Portuguese are picked off first,
before the United Nations can hear and act for (com)passionate
protections, to allow all people to keep breathable awhile longer—
can we accept environmental laws that are stronger?

As squads of children raid landfills, pull from piles of
cardboard and aluminum, glass bottles and old tires
to provide walls and roofs for moving squatters,
those climate refugees at vanguard borders,
willing to reach us from their sandy sinking islands,
blown by seasonal winds made evermore unpredictable
for farm workers, soldiers and travelers
to "faraway" places that seem to get closer by the hour.

When many congested collections of cast-offs
make cheap constructions from the dregs of our one-use
consumer society to be carried away once a year, maybe more often,
in torrential rains or fire storms never seen before
from Canada's west coast to Florida's Keys
– *is there a way we can turn back?*

"Strike Anywhere"

Proclaims red match box,
as I collect más lung smoke
made of palo santo or marijuana,
or as the Azteca say, it's just popoca.

Give me a toke and I'll be with ya
en Tokyo, when un vato Japanese-chuco says,
"Pásamelo su mecha o trola," complying,
"Simón bro, pero it ain't as safe as ama sake."

Smoke is a knot that's not easy to untie,
never an agreeable elephant
as it hooks ya with its hookah tusks
you become another soul sucka!

Ever caught your silly self, lighting up
the wrong end of a cigarette?
B-you snobby snoot crone, pug, pixie or Roman-
boned nosed, can ya lend me a match?

Yes, a magnificent match whose pungent
sulphury-potassium-chlorate competes with butane,
in its tame Zippo wick flame or dollar-store Chinese
flint wheel, offering questionable service for one season.

Unlike the "safe match," carried into battle by Imperialists,
later perfected by the French, let's applaud old ammonium
phosphate phosphorus, as the concrete jungle's war light –
used to strike anywhere, in the world's charred bazaar.

Smoking Skulls

Don't require fresh air, a tree-blessed breeze
goes unnoticed as nicotine's golden weed wraps its shadow
across teeth, gums recede as amber flecks lodge
on sour tongues, foul multi-colored smoking skulls
may take a break to chew gum.

I see bull & fawn poets whose fresh lips pucker up
for this skinny tube genie, don't realize this con-game
will beat down urban, suburban, country beauties and trolls alike;
for many have fallen before the army of shills that serve
master tobacco its daily fortune.

Ah, to be young and dumb and so full of lung!!
Food and wine's bouquet become far-away memories,
but the skulls seek bigger ash trays to go with their sipping,
so, they drag their burning butts to the vastness of the beach,
leaving mountains of filters as art of cloudy brains.

I've seen smoking skulls turn sideways and laugh at Navy Pier fireworks,
when half-mast eyes become ovals while booming jets
maneuver over the lake shore at the Air and Warfare Show,
where the tall dollars rise up all for the glory of Lockheed and Boeing,
I say I'm done with the whole lot of you – and your boneheaded smoking!

I recall when bearded beat Allen Ginsberg chanted
with cradled harmonium, "OMMM don't smoke!!"
But the bastard still smoked – as did I for another decade too long –
because at age 16, I joined my primos with sacks of Bull Durham,
cans of Bugler and Zig-Zag paper packs.

Toward the end of my addiction,
I sought American Spirits
pretending they were better
than fooling around with the militant
Turkish tobacco, Camels, Dunhill's, Murattis.

I would walk a mile for a sly Gitanes'
silhouetted gypsy dancer on pale blue box
at la casa de poeta who made pyramids
with his cigarette's ashes
while doctoring his CTA transfers.

There was a time I would have
organized my whole morning around
espresso and French Gauloises it was so *malbouffe—*
I still smell the stink of all of that
and those beret-wearing smoking skulls

Keep sucking & blowing out
ammonia, urea, arsenic, cadmium and formaldehyde,
killing us in second or first-hand cow dung clouds.
Oh, Big Daddy Wrigley, sell us more gum,
as we meditate on desires to be free of nicotine –

We need a patch, acupuncture or hypnosis
to find the best answer to our smoking psychosis, yes,
that ought to make us good for a while –
maybe we will learn smile again, as we figure out
our medical files marked: Nose, Throat or Lung Cancer.

The Gambler

October 1, 2017, Las Vegas

I.
Man leans out from luxury curtains, a good window –
opens to light and darkness straddling western vista,
his hat matching the leather seats,
what was out-of-sight, now in focus.

Moving mass, some stampede as the long guns
promise guaranteed rewards
even for inexperienced shooters—
all passengers on black locomotive,

A culling of unsuspecting bullet-ridden buffalo
slaughter, entertainment for rich,
white 19th Century travelers in their comfortable
coal and wood burners,

Churning acrid smoke across the horizon,
as elegant weapons unloaded ammo weight,
made possible by land speculation wealth
where brass-skinned people roamed.

II.
Far from sweet grass buffalo prairies,
in the neon gambler's paradise,
a lone elevator went up,
loaded down with luggage,

Opened up on the 32nd floor suite,
music muffled inside his carpeted perch,
those were not fireworks that roared out
in rapid succession,

Metal rain pierces settler's descendants
who moments earlier swayed and danced
in the warm autumn night,
was the wealthy shooter hunting

Out of darkened windows,
like well-heeled gamblers and land thieves
that once rode an exclusive American train
killing for sport – and nothing more?

The Critic

The malcontent born and raised in Egypt
his middle-aged skin smelled of good spice soap
while his words made himself angry enough to cry
burning tears that dug furrows in his cheeks
yet, each drop as white as chlorine ice.

When he cleared his throat after his bout of rage
and sipped dark clove star coffee that stained
his book's opening page, "Arabian Wine,
the Hook of the Protestant, the Koffee Haus King."

He worked on a cushion, in socks, wore loose pantaloons,
wrapped his head in jute woven mud cloth and
his neck twice with silk scarfs, his days shaped the
task as he bent his back over an old writing table,
under the pre-dawn lights of Cairo that never slept.

A drawer was where he kept his finest paper and pens,
the treasures of his travel to Rome, where he met his wife,
"Peaches" was his sweet name for his blonde who had
 expertise in wines, early Fridays he brought her flowers and a fresh
baguette and whispered a shortened French phrase in her pink ear,
"Tu prends le petit déj avec moi? Want to have breakfast with me?"

After eleven, he went to the park found his croquet partner
they managed to quickly build up a sweat in the spring heat
and he lost his modest bet, it only cost him a bundle of grapes
 his pal carried off in his bicycle's basket. Returning home, the

85

writer stopped at le boutique de tabac where he restocked with
husky pale blue packs of Gauloises and Gitanes.

He took a late lunch of sliced crusty bread and sardine
topped off with Moroccan olive oil and salt,
a sprig of basil growing in the window pot
which he added to his meal, while he sheathed his parched
throat with water and lemon juice.

Once secure in his domestic solitude
he used his antique lighter, an American relic
from World War 2, he lit two evening candles;
their lambency bent in time with the local mosques'
megaphone Maghrib call to prayer,
"Allahu Akbar, Allahu Akbar...
Ashadu anna Muhammad dan Rasool Allah..."

a moment later
he opened his unfinished book,
which each season pulled
him back to when he criticized
his life with a crooked rope.

Mistaken Identity

A maroon ribbon spurts from my right nostril,
dried blood pastes my hair against my face,
left eye swells shut in socket, as a caldera of pain
blooms, leaving me blind with the crack of a bully-club.

On my side in the back of a grimy patrol car,
they pin my arms together in over-tightened handcuffs —
the goon's face near me turns to taunt,
now in rage I deliver a leather kick to his pug-nosed snout.

In response, he pushes his revolver against my head,
"Pull the trigger asshole. I won't live in a world
where shit like you exist."
He growled, "I would, but it be a mess."

At the station, I'm carried by two uniformed brutes
who dangle me above a caged barking police dog,
laughing, they say, "You were in the park, for *music*?
Open the cage, drop him in."

Momentarily, I remember the catechism story of Daniel
as he was put inside the pagans' lions' den,
as I pull my legs to my chest,
they laugh and relent.

I desperately prayed their torture wouldn't increase,
I told them, "Look, you have the wrong guy,"
and handed them my new school ID,
but the they tore it up, scattering it on the floor.

Inside I'm chained to a chair for five hours,
deprived of water, asked stupid questions,
until finding out I wasn't who they sought,
that's when they hauled me to "juvee."

A day later I was bailed out,
you might say I was one Chicano
who got to see what the Chicago's 1968
Democratic National Convention was all about.

Aguántalo/Endure It!

Cuauhtemoczin – Swooping Eagle,
the last leader fell fighting centuries ago,
it earned him artistic immortality
on Mexican currency,

And public statuary for a society
that enshrines its native royalty,
while ignoring those who currently
share his features and non-Spanish language.

Depicted as a muscular man, chiseled profile,
framed inside an eagle-beaked helmet,
Quauhtémoczin, with outstretched arm
and hand points away from his ancestral land,

Where gods first spoke with the Mexica, Anahuac –
Tenochtitlan, Coyocan, Ixtapalapa, Tabasco, Texcoco,
all of it Cuauhtémoc's last domain,
his before bearded strangers came.

In floating mountains with giant dogs
owned by pale riders
who wore iron chests to deflect
the rain of resistance obsidian.

The strangers burnt their floating houses los barcos
upon landing, closing off escape until new boats

could be built that were to carry off
all forms of Mexica wealth.

Cuauhtemoczin was captured and dragged,
along with his captain
to the Spaniard's interrogation cave,
where a large clay pot blazed.

With mesquite-heated flame,
tied down their bare soles
blackened and slowly seared off,
unless they would confess

where rooms of the sun's
"Golden excrement" glowed.
 Cuauhtemoczin's loyal captain hollered in pain,
in pain, "This unbearable!"

To which Cuauhtémoc replied, "Aguántalo,
you'll endure it! Perhaps you think
I am being bathed in warm, flower-scented water?"
Cuauhtémoc, in agony, unable to walk,

was hung before sunrise, buried in the blue jungle,
only to reappear centuries later on treasury bills
and public monuments, pointing to his still-living
people in the navel of the moon, Mexico.

Yo Homie, Mexica Tiacauh!

*Valiant one or warrior

I've seen all kinds of wild jive on high school tee shirts;
pornographic graphics, praises to those who drug traffic,
mean defamation of people from other nations,
angry tweeties and sweeties, amid shout outs to dead family,
oversized visages of villains like Al Capone, Scarface Carlitos,
el buey Marilyn Manson and CD gangsters with their gats blasting.

Occasionally brown eagle and snake over green, white and red,
school of hard knocks drop outs, Phat Farm crop pickers,
(Farmers Used to Beat Us), NASCAR cultists, supreme
surfer symbols for those that perch 1,000 miles from an ocean,
there's even el Ché with rainbow beret,
suggesting he was gay.

There are sport's insults like the Indian mascots,
political campaign slogans for schmoes
not worth the voting, and logos from South Pole,
el gringo Tommy, even Puffy's ex-mommy,
there are tee shirts for beer drinking, and tee shirts that
prove no one was thinking when they went shopping.

But why haven't I seen one with the greeting,
"*Mexica Tiacauh*" on even one pinche tee shirt?
Maybe because we don't speak *Mexican,* and Español
clashes with words prior to Mexico lindo losing its own kapullis,
that made the 15th century Spanish arsonists
happy OK, what's kapulli, you say?

That's Nahuatl or Aztecan for *school,* but maybe you
don't like *skool* or *escula* tampoco, and there's barely
a kapulli that's open while you're sleeping
in the middle of the day, but imagine what our tee shirts
could say if Nahuatl had it not been smothered
under the tongues of the foreign ones?

Mokalli Kuate could be today's "homie," carnal,
have you ever thought what this really means?
"My house is your house?" or "Mi casa es su casa"
(don't you especially love it when Anglos tell you that?)
in turn we need say, tú tierra es mi tierra,
"This land is your land, and this land is my land"
como dice el folkie Woody Guthrie,

Entonces *Mexica Tiacauh, Kah mokal mokalli* ese *kuate*!
Don't be afraid to say it! We affirm that it's our turn
to go forward, advancing as you help others.
Let's not be reduced to fragment phrases,
leaving but a few palabras to heat our chocolate
and our chili, mi estimado amigo con su cara
del nopalito, let me ask you,
tehuatzin ti Mexikatl*?

*(are you Mexican, valiant one?)

92

Beauty and the Blade

Evelyn, the girl with the Hollywood bright teeth
and impeccable skin, talks fresh out
the joint street thug-speak, having done a six-month bit
with her home-confinement boyfriend on ankle monitor.

She's worked hard to afford
perfectly manicured long fingernails
that she uses with surgical precision to pluck out
from a beat-up cereal bag three or four fruit loops at a time.

We are on the sixth-floor of Chicago's
Roberto Clemente High School,
and locally raised semi-monolingual Latinos
do their day in English with a mix of Spanish accents

that circulate el Paseo Boricua,
most claim they don't know their
parents or grandparents' homeland
"We were born & raised in Chicago,

"Near Division, near North Ave., near Grand,
near Fullerton, near Pulaski, near Milwaukee,
near the Shakespeare police station,
this is our island, our nation,

"Humboldt Park is our Capitol, it's our garden,
our place to party on a good day,
like when there's the Puerto Rican Parade."
The dry cereal eater decides to start flinging

stale neon sugar rings toward two girls
who she also calls her "bitches," once the bag is
empty and crunchy dust dots the classroom floor,
she declares in booming voice,

"The yellow puta dies the next time
I smells pussy near my Papi chulo."
The room holds its breath for a minute
as the alarm bell rings at 9 a.m.

Twenty teen tornados take to the door and fill the hall,
I stay seated and notice under a student's desk the black
and silver handle of a professional cook's chopping knife,

Damn, it's sharp. I keep it inside my own book bag
under constant surveillance and wait to see who returns.
At the end of the day, I take it home.

Daughters

"...the sons of Elohim saw that the daughters of men were beautiful" ~ Genesis 6:2

Daughters with a desire for healing some of it tied to drugs,
Daughters of powdered magnesium and spearmint gum,
Daughters the color of rain and sky date Amilcar Cabral's sons,
Daughters with gasoline-soaked tires blocking the roads at night,
Daughters with blue corn pollen sleep in an adobe hut lit by
candles of lard and beeswax and eat pecans by the sack,
Daughters of elegance, asking for directions being rudely told to -- Shut up!
Daughters in an emergency room crisis that started on the train,
Daughters on Brazilian beaches dance without shame,
Daughters in a crowded classroom work well into the night,
Daughters of Babylon's gangsters learn what colors they can wear,
Daughters in Sacramento and Tucson look for work as the economy slows,
Daughters of Juárez Maquila Workers assassinated for being a leader,
Daughters pulled out of Haiti's rubble singing a litany of earthquake songs,
Daughters of New Orleans' Katrina living in a Mardi-Gras tents,
Daughters of Invention do wiggle-worm music on hands and knees, while
Daughters of gentrification struggle with fashion pretension and sky-high rent,
Daughter of Delacroix leads her people flag raised; no blouse tames her heart,
Daughters protest worldwide their politicians' lies and theft,
Daughters of RSD, Dengue fever, and Reynaud's syndrome prepare a feast,
Daughters of Iberia sing una canción Gitana wearing Flamenco hats,
Daughters of Mexican La Villita shop but there's no one home until 9 p.m.
Daughters of Cambridge taking a barrio ride in khaki shorts and a
hoodie on,
Daughters of suburbia worried about vampires they might like, while the
Daughters of Dulcelandia are alcoholic hijas after all,
Daughters of stolen make-up kits claim it was dropped inside their purse,

Daughters of Tibetan prayer wheels, not accessories from Prada or Levi Strauss,

Daughters of equestrian maneuvers make sure you're right in the saddle,

Daughters of Hybridities answer in Catalán to questions asked in Greek,

Daughters of ambition thwarted by tests for substances in their cheeks,

Daughters of Cambodia seek asylum in Vietnam,

Daughters of Afghanistan miss the towering Buddha blasted from the walls,

Daughters of the Middle East sick of shooting, no medicine calms the mind,

Daughters of the ex-soldiers filled tubs so bruised bodies soak in Epsom salts,

Daughter of the policewoman borrows her mother's hand cuffs for the night,

Daughter of the football player leaves home with her bastard son,

Daughters in danger of failing class stay up late with cell phones glowing red,

Daughters in astrophysics stock batteries and water in light of solar flare,

Daughters of Shangri-la don't fear demon CHRONOS as he rolls out clocks,

Daughter of Canada plays her harpsichord so May's weather will soon arrive,

Daughters of Gaelic dreamingly sip wine in Wisconsin before the curtain,

Daughters of Algeria lost in the Casbah's skin this spring,

Daughters of Two-Rivers swim in uncharted regions,

Daughters of greed collect far more than they'll ever need,

Daughters of blindness lose their sun glasses as it starts to hail stones,

Daughters of the Oneida – two feathers up and one down,

Daughters of the real first nations will never give up without a fight.

Your racing neighbors

Who was the fastest?
It was a straight forward bet between
12-year-old "Jessie" and 10-year-old me.
I tied up my shoes, "Okay, I'm ready Jessie Contreras,"
win or lose I was still stuck with my sister's
Little Lotta & Donald Duck collection, while he bragged
he had stacks of the Fantastic Four & Bat Man.

At "GO!" my five-feet-three-inch frame dashed
toward his house at the end of the block, I wished
I had Mercury's winged sandals to quickly
lift my flat feet off the sidewalk.

Jess crossed at the edge of a white family's
well-manicured fetish in crab grass, I followed
closely and touched their spongy lawn, too,
crushing it under dirty white socks in worn Keds.

Mr. Neighbor and sons watched our pipsqueak intrusion
in front of their Texas ranch home, which aroused them
from their summer lethargy, moved to action like
some Wizard of Oz flying monkeys, making whoops
and screams, "Get off our lawn you dirty greaser-beaners!"
In reply, we middle-finger saluted them and kept running.

I wondered if I should have yelled back,
"Shut up blond boloney bastards!"
— then Jessie yells, "La tuya!" I doubt

those clowns had any idea what that meant,
but there's no way we'll drink cokes and pour
over his stack of comics now,
because a moment later—there's a roar,

with red engine racing, doing peel outs, they're
laughing and launching chunks of green and faded browns,
the driver shouts, "Wetbacks! SEE WHAT YOU GET!!"
Alarmed, I asked Jessie, "Where's your parents?" He replied,
"It's 3:30, they won't be back until 6—"*Bam, bam, bam!*"
There are two goons pounding the front door
and one around back by the kitchen with a baseball bat.

Jessie grabbed a 12-gauge from the hall closet
and checked for shells—opened the side window,
and pointed it at the pair still pounding "Go away!"
Both turn simultaneously, "SHOTGUN!"
which the bastard in back must have heard,
as he cut and ran, and jumped into his truck,
with three honks & yelled threat they were gone,

"Y'all going die, for we are the Knights of the KKK!"
(I think that was the first time ever hearing about them).

Catholic-school-boy style, I recited "The Lord's Prayer,"
relived they had left, and sighed a closing "amen" that we
weren't harmed -- "Not today, Satan! No, not today."
Then Jessie said, "Vato, can you believe I was just
about to ask them if I could cut their grass for a few bucks."

Human Cicada

Getting free of TV, far from drones, planes
and honking CARmageddon, away from expensive
sirens of emergencies, slow response of armed security,
the false alarms of robo-calls, fire trucks
calliopedic comings & goings.

Bee-like babble and shouts of a thousand sports bars
and bacchanal restaurants, broken howls in blues clubs
of mid-life crisis, halls with forgettable concerts,
old dive joints where the first fugue of punk music farted,
buttock-moving Banda beats Mexicans in high heels & boots,

Caribbean crowds in Bachata contortions,
contumacious school rooms always a buzz
with scheduled bells that blast,
street crews racing stop light to stop light,
non-ignorable bazooka sounds in the middle of the night.

The big booms of audio freaks
cranked to crack the ground,
sometimes I submit to jazz showcased under
a dark constellation roof, an audacious aural
feast with drums, saxophone, bass and cornets.

Other times, I just want silence,
the avalanche of daily noise starts early
and floods nearly every dimension

I find myself in, a door opens,
an order for construction—a million decibels released.

I used to be able to hear so clearly,
the drip-drops of an over-filled gutter,
a kitchen knife slicing a sandwich of apple and peanut butter,
I once heard the whisper of ants, song of a wren,
a puppy breathing.

I would love to hear all that again,
the fall of a leaf, the slush of a wave
touching a dock, my old tea pot's whistle
and family members' voices I often miss,
some sounds I'll never forget,

Children's laughter,
the kissable voice of my love.
please forgive me if I ask you to speak up,
I have this incessant ringing
in my brain, because there's no cure.

I'll try to embrace my new status,
as the human cicada,
and who knows,
maybe, one day,
you'll become one, too.

Acknowledgements

The Call of the Chupacabra anthology,
Hotfc Publishing Company,
"Chupacabra Furlough" pp. 98

The Hummingbird Review: Volume 1 No.1 winter 2009/ spring 2010
"On the King's Road" pp. 38

After Hours: a journal of Chicago writing & art Issue No. 18 Winter 2009,
"Leap Year Two Rivers" pp. 53-55

After Hours: a journal of Chicago writing & art Issue No. 36 Summer 2018
"Old Felt Hat," pp. 9

After Hours: a journal of Chicago writing & art Issue No. 42 Summer 2021,
"Calm Panic," "Mayans Over Montana," "I do my working out in a
GRUNGE GYM"
"Your Racing Neighbors," "Company Manners" "Roseland Psychic"
pp.28-41

Nahauallian Dos Anthology of Nahuatl, Aztlan Libre Press:
"Yo Homie, Mexica Tiacauh!"

14 Abriles: Poems, March Abrazo Press, Chicago, 2010:
"Daughters" pp. 5-9

El Coro Anthology, University of Mass. Press:
"The Circus" and "With Only Smoke to Cover Me"

Carlos Cumpián is the author of four poetry collections: *Coyote Sun (March Abrazo Press), Latino Rainbow (Children's Press/Scholastic Books), Armadillo Charm (Tia Chucha Press)*, and *14 Abriles: Poems*. Originally from San Antonio, Texas, he's a contributor to more than thirty poetry anthologies, readings and workshops in the Midwest and Southwest USA. Cumpián worked in public relations for the Chicago Public Library and as an editor of small press journals and books from 1982 -2012 with March Abrazo Press. He has taught creative writing and poetry through community arts organizations including the National Museum of Mexican Art, and at Columbia College Chicago and University of Illinois-Chicago, as well as English and ESL for 23 years in the Chicago Public Schools and Charter school system. His most recent essay, "Learned to Read at My Momma's Knee," appears in *With a Book in Their Hands*: *Chicano/a Readers and Readerships Across the Centuries* (University of New Mexico Press, 2014). He is currently collaborating with Charles H. Kerr Publishing Company on the Collected Poetry & Selected Art of Carlos A. Cortez Koyokuikatl.

CPSIA information can be obtained
at www.ICGtesting.com
Printed in the USA
LVHW021957280822
727054LV00004B/614

9 781889 568102